Trust Me,
We Got This!

Denese,

You inspire me.
Love your work.
Such a fan.

Many
more.
Blessings.

Bob Gumm

Trust Me,
We Got This!

9 Steps to Beat *Single Parenting* and Redefine Your Life

Bishonna Jones

SFM
SugarFree Media

Printed in the United States of America

ISBN Paperback: 978-0-692-68930-1

This book is dedicated to my beautiful and gracious children-Jaleah, Hyland, and Savannah, for allowing me to learn so much from you and for you. It is because of you that I discovered my life's purpose of saving families, as I was first charged to save my own.

This book is also dedicated to the "single parents" that desire more for their life and that of their children. You are convinced that you are more than what the stereotypes tell you. I'm here to show you that you are right.

TABLE OF CONTENTS

PART IV: ABOUT SUCCESS

YOUR MISSION
STARTS HERE...

To say this book was planted in my heart is an understatement. I had a vision of creating this book before I was actually single. Psychic? Naw. Realist? Yes. I knew my marriage was over long before the papers were filed, and the ink dried. Signing those divorce papers was like handing my children over to the authorities, to poverty, to cyclamate low standards and expectations, to countless statistics of bubbles burst and dreams unfulfilled. A child in a single parent home was sentenced to doom according to most recent studies, and I just couldn't stomach mine included in future counts. My marriage may have ended, but my babies' chance for success couldn't. So I researched, I prayed, had countless talks with myself and my ex. Regardless of what the world said, my children would have a chance. All children should have a chance.

So this book was born out of the necessity of avoidance of disparity for me and for you. SINGLE is a relationship *status*, and not a *parenting style*.

THE BOOK AND I...

I had to successfully get through the journey so I could show others how to do the same. I just think that it is so powerful that I was given this assignment that would in turn help others overcome the negatives associated with being a single parent before I began *my* own journey. I should have taken all this in as a compliment, but instead it scared me like crazy. I kept hearing, you are going to write this book and tell your story and it is going to be powerful! This is what's going to help catapult you to the next level. This is what's going to officially introduce you to the world, so be ready. Ready I was not. Do you know how much pressure that is? Me, believing that ALL of that greatness can come from this one book! What kind of book must I write for all that success to stem from it? I felt I was tasked with writing the new Bible. If I failed, everyone would know I was a phony. I believed I wouldn't be as great as I was in my visions and as the voice had confirmed in my head. My worst fear is to be deceased and have hundreds of people at my funeral forced to speak about nothing but my potential. Because everything I could have done, I didn't. People saw a legacy in me that I was too afraid to leave. Until this day, my greatest fear is to be thought great, but remembered as mediocre or average. Finally that pain caught up to me, and I had to stop running from possible failure. I knew in order to live the life of my dreams I would have to at least complete the mission to see what happened. I had to finally get to the point where I believed I was who He said I was, and I could do, what He said I could do. I had to get there because I couldn't reside another day in doubt. When you have nothing to complain about and you still feel empty, something is wrong. You are NOT living the life destined for you. You are not in your natural habitat. That's where I was, at that place.

So now I'm here with this book for you, for us. This book wasn't for me to get everything off my chest. I journal all the time. That's been done. Also, I'm an educator. I could have easily filled these pages with pie charts and graphs, and statistics from the past decade about parenting and society and what it means for our futures and our children. It would have been no problem to cite scholarly articles using the latest buzz words or communicating the hottest parenting engagement trends promoted by the White House and Harvard. I could have elaborated on how I myself was recognized by the State of Georgia's Department of Education for my own family engagement programs. I could have, but that wasn't the direction of my heart. Every ounce in me told me to write this book using my testimony as the foundation for your recovery, your reclamation, for your transformation. Did ya'll hear that? That little voice inside our head says a lot! I know mine works overtime and can come in the form of multiple people, but that's another story. I heard clearly, don't quote the White House, quote you! Tell your story and go from there. So that's what I'm doing and all for us. I'm telling my story because I know there are people out there that will see themselves in me and gather the strength, insight, and motivation they need to move forward.

THE BOOK AND YOU

Warning, I have an interesting sense of humor. I always have. The older I get, the less I desire to sugarcoat anything. What I tell you is what I tell you and many of the times it's without the fluff. This is also a great time for me to tell you that this book could have been 300 pages long. Technically, every topic I cover could have been a separate book, but I didn't feel like that, and you don't need all that. We are in the age of say it and say it quick. Half the time we don't even use words anymore. We just send pictures. And if we are really honest, we'll admit to often sending pictures of words (quotepics). Knowing this and respecting your time, I wanted to create something short and sweet based on the chunking theory. Teachers do this often. I wanted to write a book 150 pages or less with real, relevant, and results oriented information that would allow you to get it, read it, and apply it to your life. The purpose of this book is to **G**et it, **R**ead it, **A**pply it (**GRA**) and to see that it works! The objective is not to overwhelm people, but to give them just enough that they feel confident to use in a practical way. Success comes from the application of knowledge, not the acquiring of it. And since I'm in the mood to break things down, let me also divulge of this truth: YOU are the primary focus of this book, and not your children. I am going to share strategies to develop YOU which in turn will develop your parenting. That's right. To beat the odds and stereotypes associated with single parenting, we must first work on *the parent*. Another thing, this "single" in single parenting, I'm going to challenge you to drop it. Start making a conscious effort to stop using it. Every time we go around professing single parenthood, we further perpetuate the stereotype and speak permanency into a temporary situation. We are PARENTS that happen to be single. Put the stress where it belongs, on the word **parent** and not *single*. Single is my relationship status and technically really nobody's business. If I find someone today, fall in love tomorrow, and get married next week I will no longer be a single parent, but I will still be a parent. Remember, we are what we repeatedly say. You can go ahead with all that single parent talk. I'm not continuing to speak that into the universe. I told my ex he was the rough draft before the masterpiece. We have a great relationship and can joke like that. But honestly, stop doing it. We will use single parent throughout the book for the sake of the lesson, but application wise we will work on erasing it from our vocabulary. We want our representation to be connected to abundance, not lack and that's what the "single parent" stereotype does. It represents lack. Lack of time, lack of education, lack of money, lack of support, lack of motivation, lack of interest, lack of a spouse or any form of a true romantic relationship. Lack, lack, lack, lack, lack. Then you spend the majority of your time trying to defend your efforts to become more than what the title we often boast suggests. Talk about being counterproductive!

THE BREAKDOWN

This book is broken into four parts. Part I: About Me, encourages you to be reflective about your past, move beyond any hurt and bitterness, and reinvent a better self. Part II: About Us, is a look at the family (you and the kids). It's a look at what you communicate, how you communicate, and vision and plans for the future. Part III: About Them, makes us consider the village. Who's in our tribe, who's our support system and what help do we need to receive to get to the next level. Part IV: About Success, is the chance to celebrate progress and gain clarity with the next necessary steps on the journey. For best results the steps should be followed in order and repeated as needed.

In this book we are working on developing our best possible self. We are working to *redefine* who we are and what our family will become by countering the myths. We are way more than just "single parents." There will be work to do—oh yes oh yes—but nothing we can't handle. So grab your big girl pants, a pen and highlighter, put your ego in your back pocket, and let's get to work. It's time for some loving and some of it will be SugarFree. It's time to save our family by saving us first. Ready?

PART I

ABOUT ME

HOW DID I GET HERE

By three methods we may learn wisdom: First, by reflection,
which is the noblest; second, by imitation, which is the easiest;
and third by experience, which is the bitterest.

—Confucious

Who remembers the 90's powerhouse songstress from Canada, Deborah Cox? Step 1: REFLECT reminds me of an old Deborah Cox jam that I tried and failed at singing so often. Straining, I would belt out a "How did you get here" that would make the most lenient of choir directors appalled. "Nobody's s'pose to be here" I would continue. The song was filled with so much passion that one couldn't help but to feel the lyrics as they attempted to sing the tune. When we review our path in life and our road to our current state, we are often filled with similar passion, emotion, and strain. So, how *did* we get here? What was it that rocked our worlds and changed our status from partnership to solo rider? What was it that altered life's current, our high tide to sand dune? There are many routes to single, and I'm here to tell you that whichever one brought you here, that "you are not alone." By the way, I can't sing that song either.

MY STORY...

Divorce

Some may have reached this place like myself, through the legal dissolving of a marriage otherwise known as a divorce. Contrary to what modern day society may hint at, I still believe that no one gets married with the intention of divorce. Fairytales cloud our mental space from very early ages and both men and women are conditioned to believe in the happily ever after. This becomes an obsession for women later on as we are introduced to more sophisticated love stories through books, television, and film. The once knight in shining armor may now come packaged in a suit and tie, luxury vehicle or sports car. As is the mission of any loved one, his mission is the same. His mission is to sweep you off of your feet and to create a life so great that it is unimaginable without him until you are faced with the decision to live a life without him. Ironic right? And the catch here is, the life that you can live with him gone is possibly better than the life that you live with him there. Now this twist of fate is never seen in any Cinderella remake.

With around 50% of all U.S. marriages ending in divorce, it's a constant fixture in our real lives.

I remember when I met my ex-husband. I was 14 years old, a Freshman in high school, and he helped me get in the building. I was innocent, petite, and confused. He was older, edgy, and competent. He smiled and there was an immediate attraction. Until this day, I absolutely LOVE a man with a nice smile. We became friends, then started dating a year later at a Chicago airport. Believe me. This story is not short on the romantic side. We dated off and on (mostly on) from 1992-1999. We took a break and experienced some hard times 2000-2001. We reunited 2002 and got married in 2003. I married my high school sweetheart, and the world was perfect—wrong! It didn't take long before suspicion, infidelity, distrust, disgust, financial hardships, role reversals, and family took its toll on our vows. It took three kids and 10 years for us to realize the teeny boppers in love in 1992 were not the same people we were as adults and our adult versions were no longer a perfect match.

See sometimes the signs are there, but our blinders are on. It took 10 years to come to grips with what we noticed at year three. I was disappointed. I was angry. Had I just wasted 10 good years of my life on this? Do you know how hard it is to find a spouse as you approach 40? Now, I'm a woman with not one but THREE young kids that has to enter the dating game. Are you serious? Then my focus shifted from myself to my children. Oh my, I'm about to be a single mother of three. My kids are going to become products of a single parent home. I had just become a part of the divorce club, but worse than that, my children just became three of the almost twenty-five million children being raised in a single parent home in the United States. Let the stereotypes begin.

Divorced? Now replace my details with yours and voila! It's your story. I'm going out on a limb here but I am willing to believe that when you married you thought forever was a real possibility. Although your friends, neighbors, and maybe even your parents' marriage didn't make it, your union would. How did you feel when you realized that the end was near? Right. Been there, done that, am writing a book about it.

MULTIPLE ROUTES...
SAME DESTINATION

Departure

With approximately 41% children born every year to unwed mothers, it is very possible that you may be a single parent due to departure of a mate. Departure doesn't necessarily equal the abrupt exit of a significant other. It may simply mean that an unwed couple that has children has decided to part ways. Tactfulness people! Whatever the specifics may be the end result is that you are now solo with children. Solo equals you bearing the day-to-day responsibility for your children by yourself more than 50% of the time.

Decision

It is becoming more frequent to see women over 35 make the decision to become a single parent. This thought was once taboo but now often celebrated as women heroically enter parenthood alone. What drives one to this decision? Usually an undeniable biological clock. As so eloquently summed by Choice mom of two, Mikki Morrissette , "you can find true love at any age, but you can't be (become) a parent at any age. The organization Single Mothers by Choice was created out of the necessity for support for women deciding to become single mothers. At its formation in 1981, it had only eight members and now boasts thousands all over the world. Now how is that for a growing trend!

Death

Of all the detours to single, death is the one of least control or personal influence. I always gasp when people speak of an "untimely death" as if there is really an opportune time for the cessation of one's life. Would tomorrow be better? Because today is yesterday's tomorrow. This is also usually the route of least preparation. All relationship separations have a grieving process, but with death you don't get to physically make amends with the other party as part of your healing. Their departure is permanent. This adds an additional strain when working with children and teaching them how to cope as you are adjusting yourself. Some people we don't want to see. Others we can't see. When parenting solo, in that truth lies unparalleled complexities.

YOU, STRONG?

Just when the caterpillar thought the world was over,
it became a butterfly...

—Proverb

It's no secret that through trials we gain strength. But it's through the trials part that is so daunting. Let's face it, hurt...hurts. We were created to live in coexistence with our soulmates. The fact that it takes two to reproduce was not an error on the creator's part. It is because the responsibility, the support, the fortitude needed to birth and rear a child is not a task of a solo individual but a partnership, a village. This truth makes our jobs as parents in our current state that much harder. But it does not mean that it is impossible. And surely there are others before us that mastered their faith and were successful, so why should we feel any less worthy? We shouldn't, and we won't.

Okay to Cry

When I divorced I went through an emotional rollercoaster. Some days I was like "Ding, dong, the witch is gone, the witch is gone, the witch is gone. Ding Dong the wicked witch is gooooonnnnne!" And others like, " ain't no sunshine when he's gone." Oh the confusion. Wake up smiling and go to bed puffy eyes, running nose crying. But as time passed, it got easier and my emotions became less spectrum challenging to say the least. Grieving is human nature. Honestly, it's not limited to

14

humans. You ever watch an animal planet documentary and see a mother tiger mourn the death of her cub? So grieving is our nature and a natural passage of life. Give yourself time to let it out. You were invested in that relationship. You were invested in that decision. Sure it sounded GREAT at the time, but in hindsight maybe you should have weighed more options, asked more questions, been more supportive, prepared a little harder. When reflecting you will always find that time you could have done something better. It's okay. That's what we do when reflecting. We examine the what happened and disclose the what could have happened or should have happened. Reflection is so powerful because it gives us a chance to be the man or woman on the curb watching the action. The ghost from the Christmas Carole narrating our life's story. It gives us a chance to identify what we often overlook, our obvious strengths and weaknesses.

My strength is made perfect in weakness
—2 Corinthians 12:9

That reflection is yours...OWN IT!

During my time of self-evaluation after the divorce, I noticed three things quite quickly.

1. I did NOT like being alone.
2. My self-esteem had been damaged more than I cared to admit.
3. I was a kick-butt problem solver!

First up...being alone.

Okay, so I don't like to be alone. Who knew? I guess the fact that I had been in long term relationships since Kindergarten should have been a clue, but usually you don't think about loneliness until you're alone. Since I wasn't for the most part of my life, it didn't take long to discover that it sucked! Not having someone to share intimate moments with (not sexual, but intimate and there is a difference) was the worst. A girl's night out could only do so much. I was over them by the sixth month into the healing process. Sorry girls. So my weakness revealed from my divorce was that I didn't know how to cater to myself. I didn't know how to satisfy my own needs by my own means. It's so easy to get wrapped up into the demands of others that you overlook the demands of yourself. I had become dependent on someone else to make me happy and hadn't even realized it. Which in turn led to...depression.

My self-esteem had been damaged more than I cared to admit...

I sunk into a serious depression. When it initially happened, I just thought I was sad. I was struggling with balancing kids, home, and work with less mental support. But my sadness became more extreme, and I realized it didn't seem normal. But what was even scarier than that was when I realized I had been in this place before. Shortly after my son was born, I remember having bouts of unrivaled sadness. The kind that out the blue would have you balled up weeping in a bathroom corner. The kind that would have you stare into space blankly for easily 30 minutes to an hour while the baby cried, calmed itself, then cried again. Because it wanted you, but unknowingly, you wanted YOU too. The you you once were. See these emotions resurfaced after my divorce and with a vengeance. I thought I was everything that lacked. All of a sudden, the girl that went to college on an academic scholarship wasn't smart enough. The lady that once had a young child, was mid-term in her pregnancy, managing a start-up business, completing a master's degree, and doing it basically by herself because her husband worked two low-paying jobs was all of a sudden-incompetent. The high school cheerleader with the small waist and big legs, or the petite but fierce Delta stepping on the yard with a flowing bob and contagious smile that made the boys take notice was now not pretty enough. I believed this with so much conviction that when friends, family, or strangers would counter my belief with a compliment, I wouldn't graciously accept it. I, for the life of me, would not say thank you. Instead, I would counter their compliment with something halfway negative. I had no idea that I was often times making myself a target of self-sabotage. How many of you can relate? How many of you were shaken after your single defining experience that it made you question your worth, your value to this world? See reflection affords us the opportunity to recognize our gaps in life, but it also helps us recognize our bridges.

Is there a problem?

Say it with me, "I am a problem solver." Yes you are. Yes I am. Once I identified the pain I elicited upon myself, I challenged myself to change it. And guess what? It worked. As my confidence grew, I saw a change in my life as a whole. When presented with any obstacle, not just self-esteem based, I was more inclined to think out the box to meet the challenge. As the problems got more complex, I got more creative. I had rekindled the fire to my intrinsic motivation. I no longer needed someone else to get me to start. I could do that on my own. I had learned to become *intimate with myself,* but first I had to resolve some issues. We will get into that in a minute. But for now...

REFLECT:

1. What route did you take to being single with kids?

2. How has your life changed since?

3. What have you noticed about yourself from the process (Strengths and Weaknesses)?

We Will Beat and Redefine By...

REFLECTING

We will reflect on our lives with open eyes and minds knowing the truth may hurt, but is liberating. When reflecting we allow ourselves to learn from experiences. GREAT parents know that experience is one of life's best teachers. We will help our children reflect on their lives to identify habits and behaviors positive and negative. Identification of both is needed for optimal personal growth.

BUILD A BRIDGE
AND GET OVER IT

The past is your lesson.
The present is your gift.
The future is your motivation.

—Unknown

P roblem solved. How wonderful it is to hear those words. How wonderful it would be for someone to mumble them to us as we lift our hands and rejoice. A fairy god-mother with a wand or a grandmother with a gentle touch could easily do the trick. To turn back the hands of time to simpler days when a nap, glass of water, or a good meal would be enough to calm our souls and refresh our spirits. Oh what we would do for those days again that as we get older seem so far away, but are so close. Problem…solved. Now, it takes a little more. Now we've lived long enough to know not only have the problems become more complex, but the complexities are derived from our own doing. Now both the problem and solution bare our name as creator or co-creator if we choose to share the responsibility. Now we have to confess to ourselves our role in our mess. At the end of the day, we have to agree with our spirit to move on so the problem can be solved. First things first…

FACE FACTS

I wanted the divorce to be all his fault. I wanted to have the right to paint the story that I'd share with others as the victim. I was hurt and his dirt needed to be revealed to the public in an effort to maintain my innocence. In an effort to save face and receive grace from those that would surely judge me. I needed to be innocent in it all so the fact that it didn't work couldn't possibly reflect my effort or lack thereof. If it did I would be flawed. I couldn't be flawed. Even if I had a flaw, I did not want it to be easily recognizable by anyone.

When relationships go south, we have to pause and ask, what happened? You should never do this immediately as you are simply way too emotional and wounded. But when your nerves begin to settle, your head and your heart ache a little less, and the rhythm of your breathing becomes somewhat back to normal, you should ask yourself, what happened? Now we know from earlier that being reflective is therapeutic and this time we want to dive into our role in the madness. There are always three sides to every story, yours, theirs, and the truth that lies somewhere in the middle. So to unfairly examine one, does you an injustice. What I learned from my divorce was that hurt people hurt people. Familiar findings I know, but do we comprehend it? In our lives, we are the leading character, so we always have a role in thewhat happened, what coulda/shoulda happened, and what I'm glad didn't happen. Ask yourself. What was your role in your situation? What was your role in the misery?

He Had it All...

Pouring rain, 3 am in the morning, and he's just walking in from where? There was another woman. There was always another woman, just which one this time? Lisa for the life of her couldn't understand how she kept finding herself in this same situation. She should have been every man's dream. She was smart, witty, worked out religiously. She was in great shape, had a job, took care of her kids, and cooked on occasion. A win-win from her angle to say the least, so why this again? She needed this relationship to work because she already had a child from a previous union; if this failed, it would mean two children and two different fathers. A scenario she cared not to exist. As Lisa continued her story, this is what was revealed:

- Her relationships moved from casual to serious in a short period of time.

- They became physical/sexual relationships early on.
- Most began as open relationships with monogamous commitments determined later.

Now looking from the outside in it didn't take me long at all to see why her relationships didn't last. As the saying goes, "it's a lot easier looking from the stands." She was uncomfortable with her man having multiple women, but agreed to "open relationships" in the beginning. It's hard to begin something then switch gears. You've already established the norm. After evaluating the relationship, Lisa came to this conclusion. She moved too fast and didn't communicate her standards for a relationship from the beginning. That was her role in the misery. You express not, you expect not, you have not. So that's where she ended.

'Til Death Do Us...

Donte took care of the bills because that's what a man was supposed to do and Gloria reared the twins. So when Donte passed from a car accident, Gloria was at a loss. Literally and figuratively she was at a loss. She knew nothing about their family's financials. She didn't know the passwords to the online accounts, didn't know the holder of the life insurance policy, how much life insurance Donte had, if there was more than one account, any arrangements on bills. So when he passed, the household fell apart and slowly but surely the stress she felt became reflective on the kids too. Gloria is quick to tell you that there are roles in marriage and you play yours, and though she knew this information was important, she didn't expect she'd need to know it this soon. As uncomfortable as it may be, we need to know that death is the only certainty that life gives us. Gloria was now responsible for the entire household, and she quickly realized she should have been more involved in the day to day family financial handlings. That was her role in the misery. No one wants to really talk about death, but we have to in order to prepare for it. Now Gloria is faced with another major adjustment that could have been avoided and one that will take away energy from those that need her most right now, her children.

"DRAMA" FEATURING...ME!

Once I found my ex's flirty emails from an old flame in 2004, a spirit of distrust was released so strong that it would take almost 10 years to get over. So the seed was planted and the fangs came out. Oh I was mean and believed I had every right to be. According to him, it was an "almost affair," but according to my standards it WAS an affair. Almost my....... Whether the physical piece happened or not, the damage was done. So I became very skeptical of everything he did. Nothing he did from that point on was truly good enough for me. It was substandard at best even when he thought he was giving "his" best. I realized much later that that was unfair of me. Your all is always enough for the right person. So clearly, I wasn't his right person, and he wasn't mine. When we have these aha moments, we have to take it in and let people go. We weren't made for everyone, and it's okay. It doesn't mean we're damaged goods. It just means our love is not one size fits all. We need to remember this with any relationship. We are imperfectly made for the perfect imperfect person. Forgiveness is hard and can be a long drawn out tedious process. But...

Without forgiveness
life is governed by...
an endless cycle of resentment and retaliation
—Roberto Assagioli

The act of saying I'm better and being better are substantially different and so is forgiving someone else and forgiving self. In life, overall forgiveness is necessary because resentment and retaliation are not limited to others and even more painful when self-inflicted.

My role in the misery that led to my parenting solo was that I could not find the strength to support a man that had disappointed me by infidelity. Even when he attempted to rebuild his family afterward I didn't support him. I couldn't look past his past to see a possibly brighter future. All I saw from that point on was what he lacked and that constant reminder ate away at my respect for him until there was none left. It's quite easy to outgrow someone you don't respect. Was I fair in my actions? Naw, not really. Did I fight for the marriage? I did, but could have done more. But by that point, I was mentally DONE and ready to close that chapter. Now all that I'm able to admit to you now did not come into perspective overnight. No, no, no! It was a journey to get to this point. To be able to speak about this matter with such matter of factness and transparency happened with time. Remember, my initial reaction was to save face as many of you. Play the victim and let him take the heat, remember? It wasn't until I realized my life appeared to be stunted that I came into this honestly. It was many lonely, joyless nights, mood changes, and verbal outbursts at my children that got me to question the road I traveled. He was moving on, and I wasn't moving at all and that was not how the story was supposed to go. The villain goes to hell not the victim. So something was wrong. What you mean he's dating and going back to school? Yeah he was down for a while, but sure appears to be making up ground now. Meanwhile, I've gained almost 30 pounds, nearly stopped praying and dreaming, and was at a job that had become anything but fulfilling. Dating was something that the skinny girls did, so the 30 packed on pounds made that less an option. Am I speaking to anyone here? Does this sound familiar?

Time to Heal

I had to do something, and I had to do it fast. Depression was an oh too familiar fixture in my life, and he had made a comeback. And now each time he came he stayed a little longer, and a little longer, and a... So I found comfort in self-help books. Interestingly enough, I couldn't really go to church like I wanted to during the healing time. I felt that the people in church would know something if I showed up. Like they would be able to read me because my struggles would be all over my face. I wanted the reassurance that I was right and he was wrong from my friends, but I did not want the pity of strangers. I didn't need them thinking that I couldn't cope and wasn't maintaining. Didn't need them looking at me from their pedestal then turning their glares to my children and feeling sorry. So the gospel came from books, but not the Bible. I found comfort in great reads like the *Secret, Your Best Life Now, Can You Stand to Be Blessed, Take Back Your Family, On Becoming Fierce, and the Worn Out Woman* to name a few. I had to get past my bitterness before I could go to the Bible because with a closed mind, I couldn't understand it. It was too complex. So those biblical lessons crept through the pages of my selected books, and I discovered that the universe responds to energy. Good energy goes in, and good comes out and the same to be said for the reverse. I had become stunted because too much of my time was spent on hoping for a "that's what you get" moment for my hurt. I desired a karma experience. So as I'm waiting for that instance, life moved on without me and thanks to social media, I was able to see what so many others were doing…LIVING! Some people were living quite well, and I wanted some of that. I wanted to be the girl smiling on the beach with friends or having a ball in Vegas! I wanted to change my status to "engaged" or post about my new job promotion. People showing pictures of their trip overseas and I don't even have a passport. I hadn't traveled out the country since before 9/11.

Stepping in the name of...

The urge to live a better life became undeniable, and I had to fix me to do it. So I made a bold decision. I forgave him. Everything I read told me to do it and now I understood its relevance. I couldn't possibly move forward by continuing to look back. Life has a butterfly affect. So I forgave him. People are human and make mistakes. I had made plenty, including in my marriage. So I let go of waiting on revenge, on him to get his, and I accepted the fact that things didn't go as planned and that was okay. A failed relationship doesn't equal a failed life. Life goes on, and it can still be beautiful. People were making fresh starts every day, and I could do the same.

Self-Love Replaces No Love

Most importantly, I forgave myself. I stopped hating me for staying so long in something that I knew in my heart couldn't survive. For being "stupid" enough to believe in the happily ever after. I wasn't stupid, I was a romantic and still am. I forgave me for allowing myself long bouts of self-pity and defeat. I forgave myself for straying from a needed foundation to be consumed by the wicked desires of the world. I forgave myself for ignoring my passion and purpose in exchange for convenience. I remember my sister Renae calling me crying on the phone because she said she couldn't recognize me anymore. I wasn't the strong baby sister she knew. It was a cry for help y'all. It was her crying out to me to attempt to save me. But you can NEVER save someone unwilling to save themselves. You can't make someone respect their value when they don't know their worth. So I worked on me and eventually I forgave myself for losing myself in it all. The day we decide to take the first step on the journey of forgiveness is the day a new life begins. That day I started to begin my journey was the day my motivation kicked in and my oh my the possibilities became endless!

RESOLVE:

There are many different books and articles that talk about resolving problems and forgiveness in eight or more steps, but in true Bishonna fashion we are doing it in four.

- Clarify the situation.
- Take responsibility for your role in the occurrence.
- Make an action plan to move past the problem (umm... forgiveness goes here) .
- Review your plan to make sure it is realistic (realistic plans succeed!).

Time to work:

1. Clarify what the situation is/was that brought you to being single with kids.

2. What was your role in the situation?

3. What are you willing to do to move forward past this experience (be VERY specific with what you are forgiving)?

We Will Beat and Redefine By...

RESOLVING

We will stop condemning ourselves for past mistakes and accept that those dings are what create our character. We will take responsibility for our actions and not hide behind what we may perceive as *the world did to us*. Victimization is life stunting and as GREAT parents, we will not allow ourselves or children to project or accept such. In our homes we will equally promote accountability and forgiveness.

Step 3: RECLAIM

OWN YOUR GREATNESS

The most powerful leadership tool you have
is your own personal example
—John Wooden

I failed it—twice! British Lit in college I failed not once, but twice, and I was an ENGLISH major. It was just something about that class that I didn't get, but what I did like about it was Geoffrey Chaucer. There was a line in his Canterbury Tales Prologue that has forever stuck with me:

That if gold rust, what shall iron do?

The geek in me loved it because technically gold can't rust, but I got it. If your exemplar is corrupt, then what will the common do? In parenting this line has become my EVERYTHING. We are the exemplars in our home.

What we say is not nearly as important as what we model. So, here for step three: RECLAIM; we are to reclaim our place at the throne as the rightful leaders of our home. We do this with proper modeling. The only way we defeat odds and defy stereotypes is to make the odds and stereotypes the exception to the rule and not the norm. Excellence breeds excellence. Winners birth winners. If we want a land of milk and honey for our children, we must first take claim for it ourselves. Our best life will lead to their best life and not the other way around. Our best self involves living a balanced life with spirit, career, finances, relationships, and outlets all attended to and proportioned. Through this model we lead by example and redefine success.

ME, A SUCCESS?

You have money you had success. Yes, that's what I thought. I'll be the first to admit that for years I considered success to only be financial independence. If you could buy whatever you wanted without worrying about where the money was coming from, you were a success. But my have things changed. Now that I am older and wiser, I now know there is not a single definition to success and either is it tied to one entity alone. Honestly, your life right now is someone's success story. There is someone out there praying for the type of job that you have, car you drive, home you stay in, your health, and your kids—- even with their joys and woes. Please know that there is someone out there that considers the life you live to be a blessed upgrade from their own. You to them, WE to them, are a success. This bout of wisdom just shared was the result of a major humbling experience that goes a little something like...

Almost 10 years ago, I did motivational speaking around the city of Atlanta as part of a children's career day project. I had taught for years prior and done plenty of speaking. This just felt like another day on the job. I got in front of the audience of students, parents, and staff and did my thing! There was laughter filling the air, kids shouting, smiling faces, and tons of energy. I killed it! *I thought* as I left the building. It was a two day assignment, so I was pretty excited about returning the next day. To my surprise, I was pulled by the school's counselor when I arrived the following day. She smiled and said, "Hey let me talk to you for a second." *Setup*! Usually when people say that, what follows is nothing nice. She proceeds to tell me about the *complaints* that they received from parents and staff when I left. What? The parents and staff felt that I did not project what they believed to be positive representations of success. My presentation was too materialistic and money focused and did not reflect the lives *they* lived. They complained that their lives were unfairly projected as an undesirable during my "which car and house do we want" segment. The school was located in a middle class/lower working middle class area and all of my "we want to live like THIS" options were anything but. My pictures were from the lifestyles of the rich and famous! I told the kids, "Now THIS is what we are working for" because honestly, that's what I believed. I projected to them my version of success and the grown folks were hot!

I laughed at first like, are you serious? The life they were living was not that of success. Who on TV lives like that? Then I saw the seriousness in the counselor's eyes and had to rethink my position. It was at that very moment that I realized everyone did NOT have the same idea of success. This world was not built on a one size fits all mentality. Each of us has his own philosophy on what yields success. Perception is reality and perception is based on the owner's experiences and exposures. How did I not know this before? In hindsight, I see that technically I had called everyone in that school from the principal on down a sap, sucky, failure because NONE of them lived the life that I promoted as a success. I guess that's why I was turned around and told to go home.

My eyes were opened that day, and it actually helped me give myself a little slack. Our definition of success is ever evolving. It's a seasonal definition. What we once thought a success at five is not the same at 15, 25, or 55. Who knew? Now that we do know, I challenge you to dig deep. What is success to **you**? What does it look like, feel like, and what does it encompass?

SPIRIT FILLED

Does your version of success come with *peace?* You ever wonder why so many successful people meditate, pray, or connect their accomplishments to some form of spiritual reference? Our best selves will come with the maturity to realize that our gains and losses did not come at our hands alone. To obtain optimal joy in life and to become your most successful self, it is a must that we root ourselves in a spiritual foundation. Whatever you believe in, whoever you believe in is up to you. I personally believe most of us refer to the same creator by different names and our culture not our hearts determine how we praise him. But I must tell you that it is through that creator that blessings or opportunities flow.

I grew up Baptist and am a non-denominational Christian and from birth to grown all I ever was introduced to was prayer. I knew nothing about meditation until Oprah and Deepak Chopra introduced it into my life and unlike prayer, it was hard for me. With prayer, I could just talk to God. Whatever was going on around me really didn't matter. I spoke, was still for a minute, then moved on. With meditation it is different. You have to clear your mind of all distractions and this was a chore. How do you clear your mind with so much going on around you? I am a mother. I was born with the ability to hear even when not trying to listen. My mind is NEVER clear. Something is always occupying that space. For the life of me, I could not do it and until this day still sometimes struggle with it. True story. But I will keep trying because the peace I'm told that comes from it is incomparable. To become the exemplars of our home, we have to learn how to tap into our spiritual foundation for guidance and find our inner peace. A mind on overload is a mind ready to explode. Peace is priceless. Our best self has to include enrichment for our spirit through some form of prayer and meditation.

WHAT ABOUT THE MONEY?

Getting back to the money. Our society constantly promotes lifestyles of the rich and famous. You either have it or should want it, that's the message. Therefore, it is easy to lose yourself in the definition of someone else's success. Remember when six figures was considered living large? You were rich and esteemed if you had a six –figure job. Now famous reality TV stars and online personalities trump that easily. When I speak to kids these days about being doctors and lawyers, most just look at me and smile. Their favorite YouTuber makes more money than that doctor and lawyer combined and with less education. This is the truth we are up against; therefore, it is that more important to consistently set the expectations and standards at home versus allowing the media to establish them for us. I don't just want to watch a doctor on TV, I want there to be one available at the local hospital should I need one.

Turning the focus back to us, how do we view money and success? Is our current job or career choice able to place us in a position of financial independence? After all, in terms of money and success, isn't financial independence the goal? "I want to work until my dying day," said no one ever. Or at least anyone I've ever known. Ask yourself, how much money is enough for me? What will this money be used to do? Is what I'm currently doing setting us (family) up for financial success and does it make me happy? Money is less of a factor if your joy is gone. If your answer to the latter questions is a resounding YES, bravo! You my dear are on the right track. If your answer is NO, you my dear need to jump ship. But first you need a plan.

MY JOB...MY INTERNSHIP?

Yes you read it right. If your current job is not able to position you for financial freedom, we need to change how you view your job before you change your job. Remember, we are parents. We have major responsibilities and little eyes watching how we handle every situation. That *I can just quit without a plan B* gene better be recessive and saved for emergency cases only. At this level in life, we take **calculated** risks. Meaning, we think the situation through, analyze the pros and cons, and make sure our decision doesn't place unnecessary strain on nearby parties that could be affected by our decisions. Don't dare start that—just go out on faith talk. God blesses those that prepare. Remember, faith without works is dead!

Starting today, go to work every day with the mindset that your now job is an internship for your next career move. What do we know about internships? We know that they offer the opportunity to develop marketable skills, network, and are temporary. That's what your current job has now become. It has become a place for you to garner marketable skills, network, and eventually leave. All internships don't pay, but yours does. So be grateful for that plus and keep it moving. Start researching to find your next move. What's out there that you can handle with your present skillset or that may propose a welcoming challenge? What do you need to learn to do to be competitive in that field? What's the long term projection for this next move? Does the data show that it will soon be oversaturated or is there room for growth and the uniqueness that is you? Economics is about supply and demand and you will be paid accordingly.

OPTIONS AND OUTLETS

Do you have a calendar? If so, take it out and scan this month. Are most of your to do items and events child or work related? If so, we need to talk, like right now. There is no way you get to be your dream person and live your dream life if you constantly fill your days and nights with what's important to other people. I get it, I get it. You enjoy going to your child's basketball game and dance competitions. That project at work that couldn't get done Monday through Friday must now carry over to Saturday and Sunday. I understand. But these should not be your norms. There is nothing wrong with making yourself a priority. We somehow along the way have been convinced that to care for self is indeed selfish and must now be retrained. I love the oxygen mask analogy. If when in danger you do not secure your oxygen mask first, everyone you care for is at risk. Take care of you first and this includes building relationships and having outlets.

DOES MY PROFILE
HAVE A WATERMARK?

Romantic relationships can be scary business if you haven't had one in a while. It just seems the rules of dating have changed completely since most is done online. Dating with kids can be nerve wrecking too. When is a good time to introduce your kids to a potential? For these very reasons, way too many single parents I know avoid dating all together, and I a couple of years ago was one of them. I was ready, but I wasn't. I was interested in getting to know someone, but was not fully available to them. I'll just come out with it. I had too many hang-ups. I had my prototype man and if they did not fit that mode their game was DOA-Dead on Arrival. I heard none of it. I read through profiles like a human resources recruiter scanning resumes. Nope, nope, nope, potential but no college degree so, negative! I would do small talk only to bore quickly, and the few dates I did go on were pure comic relief. *Am I being punk'd?* It got depressing. I began to realize that the men that I did find appealing never reached out to me. Does my profile have a watermark that reads *mediocres are us? If you can't hold a conversation or expect me to keep it going, inbox me now.* Immediately, I went to my weight. Over the years, I have gained some weight to say the least. I'm estimating almost 70lbs since college. That's a whole fourth grader or 93 months of baby fat (my youngest is almost 8). So yeah, I went there, stayed there, justified it, and sadly went on.

Only later to discover it wasn't my weight, it was my energy. We attract what we are, not what we want. We attract what we are ready for. I wasn't really ready for much because my confidence was shaky, so I attracted men that weren't really talking about much. As soon as I became more confident in myself, my options changed. What can I say? I've attracted some pretty cool people. Love match? Not yet, but boy am I excited. Because this energy that I'm putting out now is so ridiculously amazing, I know he will be too.

When was the last time you went on a date? When is the last time you met someone whom with you could flirt and hold a grownup conversation? Are you attracting the types that you want? Have you evaluated your energy? Or are you hiding behind the, *I'm too busy circling the world with my kids* as your excuse for exploring intimacy. Intimacy does not equal sex and neither does saying yes to an occasional date. Sometimes the company is what you need and a welcomed change.

GET A LIFE, NO REALLY...

All relationships don't have to be romantic, especially if the romantic stuff scares you right now scaredy cat. Relationships can be purely platonic and tons of fun. Go hang out with the girls or the guys. It's that bonding time with other adults that we need. When you are around kids all day, your social skills with adults decreases. I promise you. I'm sure I can find a study on that somewhere because it has to be a proven truth.

We become a little awkward, and we don't want you to be awkward now do we. So outlets should always be options. Happiness is a huge part of becoming our best self. Find what makes you happy and do more of it. If you enjoy painting, take a painting class. Like dancing? Maybe attend a ballroom dancing event where you can get all dressed up. Theatre your thing? Live shows it is. Whatever gives you that spark make room in your life to do more of it.

I realized that I have missed the opportunity to travel and have caught the traveling bug. I want to go to as many places as possible. Sometimes I bring the kids, sometimes I don't. Last month I needed a change of scenery to get some writing done. I didn't feel like traveling far, so I ventured two hours away and took myself on a writer's retreat. It was me, myself, and I on the hotel patio with the sun shining, the wind blowing, and the laptop keys a clacking. Later it was me, myself and I on my room's balcony, with room service, dessert included, enjoying the night air as I took a break from writing. I enjoyed my own company all weekend and would do it again in a heartbeat. The only schedule I was on was my own. Our children usually have a million things going on for them (clubs, classes, sports, parties), what do you have going on for you?

STEP 3: RECLAIM

A Better YOU equals a Better THEM. You define success and you alone shape your legacy.

Time to work:

1. What is your definition of success?

2. How will you keep your spirit grounded?

3. How much money is enough and what will you do with it?

4. Are you satisfied with your current job/career? If no, what changes will you make and when?

5. Do you have options and outlets (romantic/non-romantic/hobbies and interests)? How often do you engage in these activities?

We Will Beat and Redefine By...

RECLAIMING

We will create our **own** definition of success and *stop at nothing* to get it. We will not use our kids as an excuse to be boring. We will not use the "single parent" label as a calling card for pity. We will accept taking care of self as mandatory. We will date, dance, draw, take dares, and do what makes us happy as often as possible. As GREAT parents we will teach our kids the benefits of life balance including pray hard, love hard, work hard, and play hard. They will know that it is when these things are in proportion that we are whole.

PART II

ABOUT US

Step 4: RELATE

LITTLE PEOPLE HAVE RIGHTS TOO

If you want to be trusted,
Be honest.
If you want to be honest,
Be true.
If you want to be true,
Be yourself.
—Unknown

Kids, a mess aren't they? They keep us going. Going to the school, football practice, orchestra concerts, ballet recitals, and the local wine shop depending on the circumstances. We love them and can shake them good at the same time. Packaged in those little squirmy bodies, it's sometimes easy to forget that real pint sized (super-sized if you have teenagers) people exists. Children are people with needs and wants similar to our own. It's easy to go on with life thinking no authentic explanation is desired or necessary to give to our babies about *anything* that occurs in *our* lives. To tell the truth, most parents operate in the "because I said so" or "do as I say not as I do" mode leaving explanations to stereotypical over educated upper-class elites with no control over their offspring. We are discovering in today's age that our kids have access to more information than ever before, and we need to be on the controlling and not defensive end of the conversations. In other words, we have to talk to them more and about more before the world speaks to them first.

COME CLEAN

Fess up. Have you had the why mommy and daddy aren't together talk with your kids? Have you sat them down and given them the kid-friendly version of the story? If your child is old enough to sit through a 30-minute tv show attentively, they are old enough to digest some form of that truth. Now what details you include will vary in regards to the age of the child, but certain aspects need to remain constant.

1. Parties involved (parents)
2. Decision made by parents/or what happened to the other parent
3. What the decision or the happenstance means for the child

Now when discussing the parties involved, it is very important that the focus remains on the parents and not anyone else that may have played a role. If there was a third party involved, it can be tactfully mentioned (for school-aged+kids) but should never become the focus of your conversation. Let it go. If you stick to the basic truths and leave the emotions out, the story is easier to tell, and you won't be tempted to create a hero (you) and a villain (them). Remember, children are observant. If you mess up and paint yourself as a savior and the other parent as the devil, that's a pedestal you better be prepared to stand on forever. And every time a flaw of yours is revealed, it will create a chip in your character and every time *they* do right it will be promotion to grace. The most authentic evaluations are done by observing others actions. Let's allow our children to do that to form opinions of their own.

Next, as far as the decision made or the, what happened? Be honest here too and remember there are two sides to each story. Even if the other parent is deceased, be honest about how it happened. We sugarcoat so much for the sake of saving people that we don't realize what that false sense of safety and confidence does in the future. It's a setup for eventual backfire. The truth will set you free and a lie will hold you hostage. So what's your preference?

Lastly, please remember to let the babies know that they are innocent in all of this and that they are loved regardless of anything that happened. Give constant reminders that they will always continue to be loved. As new people come into your lives, and they will, the love you (parents) have for them is unwavering. If we sit our kids down and have these kinds of real talks, these kinds of conversations, they will not have to be resentful, suspicious, or defensive as new people enter our circle. They will understand their value in our lives and know they don't have to compete to maintain it.

Girl, your kids...

I've had numerous friends and family members tell me how impressed they are with how my children have adjusted to the divorce and how my ex and I interact. That great adjustment was intentional. We did the work upfront. I made sure I NEVER spoke negatively about their father in their presence (may have had some choice words when they weren't around). This is soooooo important. You won't believe the number of parents that come into my office on the regular just bashing the other parent and often right in front of the child! I just look at them, teeth gritted, and smile. Then I dance around what I really want to say. In a school system your expression is limited, but in this medium I get to be as SugarFree as needed! So yes, to say the least, my children have adjusted to divorce well. My ex and I make a conscious effort to stay positive and cordial at all times. WE ARE A FAMILY, and divorce didn't change that. My children understand that our marriage didn't work, but our family structure will. They also get that as time goes on our family will grow because mommy is wifey material, and dad is, I guess alright too.

EMOTIONAL ROLLERCOASTER

Some may be thinking, easier said than done. But technically, the more you do something the easier it becomes. Getting started is what's important right now. All children aren't going to instantly adjust. Mine didn't instantly adjust. We got to this place over time. We are emotional creatures and children are no different. Our role as the parent is to let them experience the highs and lows. Let them get it out their system and know it's human to react that way. Validate them with "it's okay." Emotional growth is just as important as our other growths be it physical, spiritual, financial, and etcetera. Let them get on the emotional rollercoaster and build their tolerance and character.

Speak to your kids and ask them questions. Being with only one parent may be new or something they've done for years. Check in on them. Find out how they are coping. See if they have any questions. I asked my kids were there any pros and cons of the situation and they were quick to tell me yes. They got to have three Christmases! One at home, one at dad's house, and one at Grandma C's house (dad's girlfriend's mom). I chuckled. I guess that would be a positive. Look, if your ex is able to move on and meet someone that genuinely cares for your kids and treats them well, put your pride aside and accept them. Better yet, pick one of those high ticket items off that

Christmas list and assign it to them! #Welcometotheteam. They can help **you** out! Always be an optimist and never a pessimist. Find the good in it people, find the good in it.

Whether being a single parent is new to you, or you've done it for years, our job is to be the constant, be the structure, be the high-five when they are happy and the hug when they are sad. Our job is to be the "but I still love you" when they are angry or in the wrong. Children crave structure and our role as the parent is to supply it.

Let them speak...

"Kids have rights too!" I recall my oldest saying as she looked me in the eyes with confidence that made me proud but almost offended. Was this little girl challenging me? Oh wait a minute! I felt my pressure rising as the older folks say. I had to gather my composure before I spoke. "You're right, kids do have rights. But in this house..." And that did it. I saw her little spirit just as broken as she came to the realization that her mother was a hypocrite. I had done all this talking about speaking your mind and being able to stand up for yourself, advocate for yourself, and when my child attempted to follow my very advice, I shut her down, and I saw it. I saw it in her eyes. I had to fix it because if I didn't, those lines of open communication I pride myself on would slowly but surely no longer exist. Why? Because I just made speaking your mind uncomfortable. So I back paddled. I tried to unsuccessfully explain my way out of it. Then I finally decided to do what I should have the first time. Let the girl explain. Let her present her case. Let her speak. One thing you need to know about my oldest Jaleah, is that she is never at a loss for words (gets it from her mama). She is a sweetheart and needs a t-shirt that reads *One Day I'll Save the World*, but she is not afraid to speak her mind to anyone. I decided to listen, and what I discovered was I had been shutting my kids down. I had been very short with them, and they were feeling the strain. All the "we we we" that I preach had become "me me me" and my kids were feeling slighted. I had to take ownership of it. They were right! I was stressed at work and feeling stunted in life, and they were the victims of my wrath. During that time, I was also going through a personal pity party because it appeared their dad was moving on, and I wasn't moving at all. Adjustments aren't one time things, but ongoing. As they were adjusting, so was I. Open lines of communication are important in every relationship including ones with our kids even if what they say may burn to the core. Hey, the truth hurts and kids don't have filters.

Now lean back

After being humbled by my daughter, I reassessed my then current situation and realized I needed my kids to be my support system just like they needed me. Please don't be confused. It was a hierarchy system with me at the top and power not spread equally. But we all had vital roles to play. With life comes struggle. That's a fact. But struggle doesn't have to be done in solitary. Lean on each other for support and draw from each other's strengths.

It is very important that parents allow children to see both struggle and progress, for they are natural occurrences that coexist in life. To shield one from hardships, will leave them ill prepared to handle such strife.

STEP 4: RELATE

Be open. Be honest. Be intentional. Set the tone, but be flexible. Above all, be receptive. And this my friend, will speak volumes.

Time to work:

1. Have you had the why mommy and daddy aren't together talk? If no, when will you have it?

2. Does your child have a "voice" in your home? How can you tell (examples)?

3. When it comes to family chats, do you normally initiate the conversation or the child?

4. Are you open and honest in dialogue with your child about past and current situations or do you try to save face?

5. What one thing will you initiate immediately to relate to your child better and create open lines of communication?

We Will Beat and Redefine By...

RELATING

We will exchange open and honest dialogue with our children and give ourselves permission to appear flawed. We will simplify content for their understanding and elaborate as they mature. We will always remind our children of their voice in and out the home and the importance in finding comfort to use it. We will communicate failure as a rite of passage for success. As GREAT parents we will encourage our children to identify and release their emotions as a natural progression of internal growth. Through it all we will remain—supportive.

Step 5: REIMAGINE

OH THE POSSIBILITIES

The world is but a canvas to the imagination
—Henry David Thoreau

Pharrell Williams is one of my favorite artists of all time. Not just because I love his funky get ups and am surprised by his wardrobe selection at every award show. Not just because he can go from producing music, to singing, to writing and producing movies, author, designer, and slowly becoming a business icon with his trendsetting deals. But because he is never afraid to think outside the box. He is never afraid to venture into the unknown for the potential joy that comes from "it worked!" So when his 2014 single *Happy* hit the airwaves and became an instant hit, I was overjoyed. One because, I'm a Pharrell fan, and two because how cool was it for a song about being plain old HAPPY to be received by so many. In a world where projects about sex, drugs, and violence leave empty shelves and sold-out theatres, a song about innocent joy could carve a niche and climb to the #1 spot over and over again all around the globe. I guess that was just a little proof that no matter how hectic this world gets, at the end of the day, we all just want to be—happy.

ASSESS THE HAPPY

What makes you happy? What makes you truly happy? Actually better yet, what makes the family happy? Now that we've had a chance to level with our children by speaking to them open and honestly, we can move on to the next step which is reimagining the possibilities. What is your short term and long term vision for the family? How do you discover your *happy*? Ask the kids what do they enjoy doing when no one is watching? What do they enjoy most when everyone is together? Think back to fun times shared and assess. What were you doing when those memories were being made? What brings you and them joy?

When I took the time to do this exercise, I noticed right off that my rugrats like to go! They like to be out and about. I can tell them to jump in the car and let's go for a ride. Better yet, jump in the car and let's go on a road trip! My bunch loves to travel. It's something about staying in a hotel that makes them feel all fancy. I also noticed that they love the outdoors and enjoy parks and beaches. The parks I'm good with, but the beach scares me a little because the first thing they want to do is go by the water. We can't swim! "We" as in none of us. My son can do that fake swim thing, but I'll never put him in the deep end to test his skills. So in that case the beach makes them ecstatic and can make me a nervous wreck, but I'm a team player so I'll go.

SET A VISION AND MAKE IT CLEAR

Now take what makes the family happy and give it legs. For the next year, plan on doing more of what gives you energy and satisfaction. Be specific. What will you do and how often will you do it? You are going to use this information to create a family vision board. Vision boards are very popular these days and most consider doing them as individual projects, but I also suggest that you do one as a family. Make sure to include activities that you have always wanted to do but have never tried for extra excitement. I like to include a fear to overcome to help continue to move us past our comfort zone. There's no growth in comfort.

This year, we did a combo board (individual/family) and on it we have swimming. It was a no brainer. I have a love hate relationship with water and my kids can't get out of it. For sanity purposes, we all must learn how to swim this year. A fear of mine is being in a car that somehow goes into water and there is nothing I can do about it. I'm just there like "take me now Lord" because even if I could get out the car I am still doomed. So swimming it is. My son Hyland is really interested in football and wants to play this year;

so, that's on the board. I'm not crazy about my baby getting hit and am trying to encourage him to be the kicker, but it's not working. My oldest daughter Jaleah is super creative and wants to publish a book she's been working on since last year; so, that's on the board. My youngest daughter Savannah is full of energy and was quick to tell us that she has never been to the circus. Well, find the picture and grab the glue stick. The circus it is! We also added some school related goals, vacation spots, dining options and a 5K to get the family moving. I am proud to say that our board turned out quite nice, and we have been making some decent progress on getting through it.

ALL GOALS CAN'T BE TOUCHED

One note to consider is that of long and short term goals. A year is not a long time, but we can still chunk it into shorter time frames like quarters or months. My family and I often do separate vision or goal boards on a dry erase board that we keep downstairs. This board changes frequently. If there is something we have to focus on for the week, it's a week goal board. If it's something we are working on for the month or quarter, it's a month or quarter board. Right now we each have two goals to meet and 5 weeks to do it. One of my goals is to finish writing my first book. If we are all successful in meeting our goal, we get two days at the beach! Remember how my crew loves staying in hotels and the beach. We are off for two days if our goals are met. Please know that carrot at the end of the stick is working, and we'll be at the beach in no time flat.

Some goals you may put on your board may not be as tangible as others. My oldest daughter felt we were drifting away from church, we hadn't been attending as often (guess my live streaming service didn't count) and wanted us to go more and strengthen our faith. Going to church more was measureable, but strengthening one's faith was not as tangible. But it became a goal none the less. My son noticed his confidence has been shaken this year and his spirit challenged (mama noticed that too) so he wanted to have a goal of increasing his confidence. How awesome is it when you have children so reflective that they can identify strengths and weaknesses within themselves and are willing to work on them both! I tell you I am one proud mama. There is absolutely no motivation better than intrinsic motivation. You have to want better for yourself more than anyone wants it for you. These boards are powerful and in our household they have made a difference.

WILDEST DREAMS

Something else I like to include on the board are things from your wildest dreams. If life goes exactly as planned, what would it look like? What's an outrageous dream thing you have and put it there? Now these goals will take longer than a year and will require much assistance from outside sources. Not a problem. Start planning and recruiting now. My kids have a cousin that was homeschooled for years and absolutely loved it. Guess what? Homeschooling is one of their wildest dreams at the moment. My vision of sitting on an island resort sipping a mojito as I pen my next New York Times Best Seller evidently has them next to me sipping on a Capri Sun doing Algebra homework! Umm, not too sure about that one. Their wildest dream is now imposing on mine. As parents, we have the right to be selfish in moderation. They might have to rethink that one. "Hey kids, what's your wildest dream... #2?"

TEAMWORK MAKES THE...

Boards are done. Check. Time to assign roles and accountability. Who is going to be responsible for what? Individual goals were an easy fix. The individual that selected the goal is responsible for it and everyone else is their accountability partner. The family goals, however, needed a name attached to each. This is not done randomly. Do it based on each family member's strongest skill (or a weakness that you present to them as a strength to help them build it...tricky parents) and share with them why they were selected for the role. For example, my oldest is the most spiritual of the group and therefore she was in charge of our faith building goal. My son can be a bit of a perfectionist in some areas which can cause him to move as slow as molasses, so he became our time keeper. It's working rather nicely. Remember that confidence building goal? Well every day we leave the house on time, guess who gets the credit? Exactly.

ROADMAP READY

All organizations be it a school, church, or business have both a vision and mission statement. Your family is a structured organization. It's the most significant piece of your legacy and in many ways must be handled like a business. We need a family vision and mission statement to keep all parties focused and proceeding in the same direction.

A vision statement speaks to the future and a mission statement speaks of the present. Your vision statement will describe what the family wants to be in the future. The mission statement outlines what the family will do now to prepare for that future. For example, our family vision statement is:

Colbert-Jones Family Vision Statement:

To fulfill our life's purpose by doing God's will and living the most fabulous regret-free life possible.

Colbert-Jones Family Mission Statement:

In this house we will...

Take chances, say I love you, laugh loudly, learn from mistakes, have fun, do our best, forgive others, pray often, and believe that anything is possible.

You may have seen the "In this house" plaques at your favorite shopping spot. I so love them and many speak to my heart, but I can't have them all so I created my own. My children are all under 13 so an elaborate vision and mission statement aren't necessary. I believe these do the job just fine. Now when you create your vision and mission statements, be sure to frame them. It makes them look official. One cute idea I saw was a hand print added as a signature. How adorable! How creative you get is completely up to you. Make sure what you decide speaks to who you are and what you're becoming.

STEP 5: REIMAGINE

We are only limited by our imaginations. Imagine the best life possible for your family, then go out and create it!

Time to work:

1. What makes your family happy?

2. What are some of your family goals for this year? Individual goals?

3. Which family member can be assigned to each goal?

4. What are some of your Wildest Dreams goals? Who and what will you need to help get you there?

5. What is your family's vision statement?

6. What is your family's mission statement?

We Will Beat and Redefine By...

REIMAGINING

We will dare to live our wildest dreams! We will brainstorm as a family ways to improve our existence individually and collectively. We will challenge ourselves to face and overcome our fears. We will have a mission and a plan to make it so. As a family we will hold each other accountable for our vision and the role each plays to make it true.

PART III
ABOUT THEM

WANTED: TRIBE MEMBERS

Call it a Clan,
Call it a Network,
Call it a Tribe,
Call it a Family.
Whatever you call it,
Whoever you are,
YOU NEED ONE.
—Jane Howard

od is Good! I can't help but think as I sit at the desk in my plush leather chair allowing the spring breeze to hit my face. See, my house is silent except for the tapping of my keyboard, birds chirping, humming of cars passing in the distance, and the occasional neighbor's garage door opening for their entry or exit. Those few distractions are nothing when you are use to the daily noise of three children coming and going to the point of exhaustion. Well, my three aren't home this weekend. Usually they aren't home every other weekend because they are with their father. With their father can be interpreted as with dad, or with dad and grandma, or with dad, grandma, and papa, or with dad, grandma and papa, Ms. Mel, and...you get the point. I can exhale now knowing my children are okay. Knowing they are safe, I can now do more of what I like and find time to take care of me. The weekends without the kids have become a time to destress, and we all need to destress. The challenges of the world can prove to be too much to manage and an outlet is not only necessary, but mandatory for complete balance of our mind, body, and spirit. When you are parenting solo, it may be hard to find those outlets. But from my years of research and discovery, I now know most of those difficulties are self- inflicted. If you didn't know before becoming a "single parent" that navigation through this world is impossible alone, well you know...

SUPERHERO COMPLEX

Getting here took time. Getting to the place where I could relax while my babies were in someone else's care took time. So give yourself the opportunity to detach. I had to remember that these little ones are the same little ones that grew in my womb for almost a year. That the umbilical cord that fed them for months was replaced by a breast, a bottle, a spoon and fork, a touch, and a smile. The connection between a parent and child is undeniably strong and the urge to protect our young is a natural instinct. So when we find ourselves trying to do it all for thinking no one can do it like us, that too is natural. But natural doesn't always equal best. Superheroes are fictional characters for a reason so abandon the desire to become one.

Burn, Baby Burn...

You will absolutely burn yourself OUT by trying to raise a child alone. Life is demanding, yours and theirs. To manage your own is a task, now we are responsible for the daily management of another? Even the most organized, multi-tasking parents can't beat this odd. If all of you is not enough for you to live a successful life, how will it be enough once you divide your time and efforts amongst others? Simple math says it won't work. I've heard the stories, authored quite a few myself: I don't have anyone near me to support me, the father (mother) won't help, I don't have enough money, people don't have time to help me with my kids they have "xyz" going on, and blah blah blah blah.

These are the scripts we rehearse in our heads for quick recital once we look completely beat down and someone asks us about our present condition. It's the single parent playbook for pity. We usually follow up our first excuse for looking exhausted and spirit drained with a counter punch. We'll say something that makes us look amazing. We'll spurt a how do they do it all type of response. This is our superhero resume.

Things like: I'm working two jobs, back in school, finishing up "xyz", starting my own…, about to… And it works! People are astonished by our strength and pure tenacity. "Because I want my kids to have better, be better…" is the closer that leaves those that doubted us with nothing but hope because we…are…doing the darn thang! Or are we? From the outside looking in we may be, but from the inside looking out we definitely are not. We're tired. We're stressed, and stress can kill you. What type of better life will that be for our children? Say it with me…We Need Help. Parenting was not meant to be a solo endeavor.

WHAT DO I NEED?

Finding your tribe is all the rage right now. There's a plethora of books by bestselling authors about the necessity of surrounding yourself with like minds for optimal personal growth. This idea, however, is nothing new. The Proverbs: "You are the company you keep" or "It takes a village to raise a child" blends in perfectly here. So it's time to find your tribe, your team, or recruit new members if you have one already.

Questions

Before you can recruit a team you have to have a vision for the team, or a purpose. You have to outline roles of the players involved. To do any of this, you first have to ask yourself some hard questions. What type of life do I want for myself? For my children? What do I do well for self? What do I do well for my family? What do I have enough of? What am I lacking? Every answer should relate directly to the type of life we want for ourselves and family. So the answer to "what am I lacking" is going to reference what we are lacking to live purposeful, fulfilling, successful lives as an individual and as a family. Get it? What or who are my resources? Who or what can help me/us move forward? Do I know where to find more resources? If our life was unbelievably fantastic, what would it look like? What help do we need getting there?

Roll Call

Who here has played kickball? Remember being on the playground lined up excited because the captains were about to start selection. Remember the excitement you felt when you were the captain making the selections. It was sooo hard! You had a limited amount of time to access everyone's skillset to create your dream team. Often things were further complicated when you had more friends than spots, or your friends weren't the most athletic in the bunch. Remember that? You had to then begin to think like a leader and recall the necessary attributes needed to win the game versus keeping the peace. It was business, nothing personal, and eventually everyone got beyond their feelings.

When recruiting for our tribe, we need to go back to those days and reignite that energy and purpose. In this game of life, we came to win and to win we need a solid team. This is nothing personal. Some people will be key members of your tribe while others are a support group. After gaining a clearer picture of your ideal life through questioning, you are ready to start recruiting. The size of your tribe is completely up to you, but there are six key roles you need to fill: the co-parent (family), the nurturer, the role model (mentor), the gap filler, the truth seeker, and the cheerleader.

TRIBE MEMBER PROFILES

Co-Parent/Family

If the other parent is alive and and not a safety concern for the children, let them be a part of the children's lives. We resolved our differences and rid ourselves of bitterness regarding them in step 2:RESOLVE. Now it is time to co-parent like a champ! I am here to tell you that my ex Jerry and I co-parent 20x better now that we are divorced than we EVER did while married. You will do more damage than good by keeping the biological parent away from the child. Even if the other parent does not show what you consider to be enough effort, you make the effort to get them involved. That extra step that you take now will benefit your child later.

It's easy to be selfish if the relationship with the other parent ended on a sour note, but remove yourself from the equation. Once you had children your relationship was no longer about just you. Once the relationship ended, it became ALL about them. A revenge mentality has hurt more families than we care to count, and there's no need for us to add to the numbers. It is that parent's biological right to be a part of your children's lives whether you like it or not. If due to circumstances the other biological parent is not available, it is important to connect with one of their family members. It is best if our children see representation from both sides of the family in order to feel whole. I have conferenced with at least 100 parents over my 13 years in education about this matter and the effects of family distancing on children's self-worth.

It is easier to build
Strong children,
Than to repair
Broken Men
—Frederick Douglass

Children understand that two parts make a whole and while we can be overwhelmingly loving and caring, we can never replace the other part. So for the sake of the child, make every effort to include in their lives the biological parent or someone from their family to avoid a potential identity crisis or longing for a relationship with people they never had the opportunity to know. Our goal is always to create completeness, not voids.

Nurturer

Let me guess; no one takes better care of your children than you? Most of us feel this way and for good reason. However, we can't be everywhere all the time; so we better find some extra hands to trust. Life happens, and it's okay. I am fortunate enough to have a close relationship with my siblings, parents, and ex-in-laws. If my or my ex's schedule gets hectic and we can't get the kids from school, make a conference, a dance recital or football game, we have backup. We have people we can trust with our children's lives.

The role of the nurturer is to be the caregiver for your children in your absence. This absence may be temporary due to schedule conflicts and emergencies, or this absence may become more permanent in case of death. Your nurturer is your replacement. It's always a good idea to recruit your nurturer based on the long term and not the immediate. Who could fill your shoes if needed? You recruit this person for your tribe early to give your children a chance to bond with them. My older sister Carla is my main nurturer although I have multiples. She resides fairly close, maintains stable relationships, and lives a lifestyle similar (actually an upgrade) to my own. To me, lifestyle includes spiritual/ religious/ educational beliefs, pastime activities, and socio-economic status. I approve of her heart and her lifestyle and therefore feel comfortable with her filling my role if needed. What qualities are necessary for your nurturer? Do you have a nurturer in your tribe?

Role Models/Mentors

Who do you look up to as a trusted leader in your field? Who do you know that has the image that you desire? Who embodies the checklist of what you want your daughter or son to be? Who?

Role Model=

> **Dictionary.com:** A person who serves as an example of the values, attitudes, and behaviors associated with a **role**. For example, a father is a **role model** for his sons.
>
> **Merriam-Webster's Dictionary:** someone who another person admires and tries to be like. A person whose behavior in a particular role is imitated by others.
>
> **Wikipedia:** a person whose *behavior*, example, or success is or can be emulated by others, especially by younger people.

The next person/people we need in our tribe are role models and mentors. A *role model* is a term commonly associated with people we admire and imitate in our youth, but as we age we discover that there still is a need for their existence. The more grown-up and modern term for a role model is a *mentor*. Usually there is a more tangible aspect that is associated with mentors and mentorship. However you decide to look at it, we need them. It's important to *hitch our wagon to a star* and learn as we go.

When searching for role models and mentors we need to keep two separate focuses. Who is good for us? Who is good for the kids? We have to surround our family with exemplars of success. People naturally imitate others, so why not imitate the best? Role models and mentors challenge us to go beyond our comfort zones and grow. When we place the end result in front of our children to see it's attainable, it becomes our family standard. It becomes the norm for them. Think about it. Children born into wealthy families never worry about being rich. Being rich is their norm, how rich is their decision. There is a difference. So find role models and mentors for yourself and your children to elevate your norm, your standard, your quality of present and future life.

Gap- Fillers

The running joke in my family is if the party starts at 6 o'clock, tell me five. I hate to say it but, time and I have a love hate relationship. I love it and want more of it and hate that it ain't gonna happen. We all get the same 24 hours a day to be productive, and those with good intentions don't get an extra hour for effort. Every self-help book I read stresses the importance of being timely, and this is a battle I've fought ALL my life. You wouldn't believe the number of weddings and graduations I've missed (or partially missed) due to mismanagement of time. Flaw alert: I have the horrible habit of trying to do too much at once. It's not that I can't complete the tasks, it's just that I can't complete *all of them* at the same time. I am a work in progress I tell ya. If I plan to experience optimal personal and professional growth I have to overcome this issue. To do so I've elicited help. I had to find a few good gap-fillers.

Each relationship nurtures a strength
Or weakness within you
—Mike Murdock

The role of the gap-filler in your tribe is to *be the strength where you are weak.* People are the sum of a multitude of puzzle pieces. Each personal trait and experience that we have is a piece of the puzzle that adds to our character. As we know from Lao Tzu, *character becomes your destiny.* My older sister Renae and my son Hyland are my present gap-fillers for time management. They are both textbook type "A" personalities and perfect accountability partners because I can't stand the wrath that comes from them.

Gap-fillers are necessary for personal and business growth. Creativity is a definite strength of mine, but time management isn't. For this reason, I had to turn over many marketing development components to others (logo, web design, video production, and etc). It's not that I couldn't do it, or didn't try (I was actually looking into enrolling in a graphic design class so I could make my own marketing material-lol), I just had to realize that it was a job that someone else could do. I remember hearing Lisa Nichols say, "Focus your time and energy on doing what only YOU can do." Well only I can tell my story like me, so my time had to go into telling my story and not into developing marketing material and book editing, and etc. Make sense? So what are your weaknesses and who can you recruit to fill in the gaps to enable you to propel forward?

Truth Seeker

The people that we need the most and want to see the least are the tribe's Truth Seekers. The Truth Seeker's role is to do just that; seek the truth from you and not sugar coat what they see. So often we share ideas with family and friends only to receive raving reviews. When things go south, we hear, "well I knew it wouldn't work," or "I wanted to tell you but wasn't sure if you would listen." We've all had these experiences I'm sure. Well, in our tribe we need those that will (as the kids say) keep it 100%. They will tell us the truth even when the truth is not what we care to hear. Self -reflection is helpful, but it is restricted by our imposed mental limits.

"Sometimes you can see better from the curb," I remember my mother saying. As an adult, I now understand. Sometimes you can see a situation better when you are removed from the situation like a third person narrator is able to see all sides of the story and report from that angle. This is what the Truth Seeker does and their presence is vital to our success. My brother Lamont is one of my truth seekers and spiritual guides. When he breaks it down for me, he does so according to the world and the word from the perspective of man and from God. I don't always want to hear what he has to say, but I listen. Truth comes in many forms and sometimes it's from personal experiences and lessons learned, and sometimes it could be from people and *their* lessons learned. So whoever you pray to, whatever you believe in, ask for a spirit of discernment so that when a truth seeker presents himself to you, you are open enough to receive them and their message.

Cheerleader

Have you ever met someone that believed in you more than you believed in you? Other than your kids of course. Well I have. Many times over. But my biggest cheerleader of all has to be my oldest sister Lynette (Nette). The last key person we need in our tribe is the cheerleader. The cheerleader's role is to be your energy when you have none. They are constant motivation. From your subconscious mind they are the angel (your fears and doubts are the devil). Somehow my sister believes there are only two people that can walk on water, me and Jesus. How she arrived to this, I'm not sure. But to say she is proud of her baby sister is an understatement and her sheer *enthusiasm* for my life is like nothing I could have ever imagined. And I can imagine a lot! We always need people in our corner that will hoorah us on to the next level. We need people that remind us of how far we've come and not just how far we have to travel. As you recruit for your tribe, look for that person with the constant optimistic view. Look for the problem solver, the solution giver, the we "can" instead of we "can't." Seek the person that has an honest interest in your latest adventures and hold them tight. We always need them down the road for this journey to our best selves.

Where do we find these people?

Ready? Look up, look down, look right, look left. These people are all around. Our future tribe members are all around. Some may be in your family, some may be your friends, co-workers, fellow church parishioners, classmates, someone you met at a workshop or online support group. They are literally everywhere. Our job is to qualify who we see. We do this by asking the necessary questions in the beginning. What do we need help with to become our ultimate self? Our ultimate family? Then we observe those around us to see if they can fill our vacancies. If you don't see anyone in your immediate circle that can fill the gap, then enlarge your circle! Network with others to achieve the necessary results. Anyone that knows me knows that I am a Steve Harvey fanatic. His story, his approach to life, and his success appeals to me. He may not be as tangible as I need him to be at the moment, but thanks to the internet, I can still have him as a mentor. There's no rule against virtual tribe members-lol! So stop where you are and look around. Is there anyone qualified to join your tribe? Are there success minded individuals available to recruit?

RECRUIT:

No one makes it in life alone. You are only as good as the team you build. Who's on your team? Who's in your tribe?

Time to Work:

(Give yourself time to think through the answers. Skip hard ones and come back to them after you've had more time to think. The key is to COME BACK and complete the work.)

1. If my life was unbelievably fantastic, what would it look like?

2. What help do I need in creating that fab life for my family?

3. What resources am I lacking and how can I get access to them?

4. Is the other parent active in my child's life as a co-parent? Does my child have a constant representation from the other side of the family? If not, what am I going to do (go the extra mile) to change this?

5. What qualities does my nurturer need? Who is my nurturer?

6. Who are possible role models for my child(ren)? Who are possible mentors for me? How do I make these people accessible?

7. What are three of my main weaknesses? Who does well what I don't and can fill my gaps/gap-filler?

8. Who is my truth seeker? Am I completely honest with this person?

9. Who is my cheerleader?

10. Where can I go to find additional resources to build my tribe and support me on this journey? When am I going to do this? The answer to this question should always be now!

We Will Beat and Redefine By...

RECRUITING

We will seek help where help is needed. We will inventory our life for strengths and weaknesses and recruit the latter. We will accept that it takes a village to raise a child, and the single parent superhero myth is overrated. We will take time to assess what we need in order to know who is a fit for our tribe. As GREAT parents we will defame the idea of a *self-made* success story, and teach our children the benefits of networking and relationship building.

JUST SAY "YES"

YOU are not a burden.
You HAVE a burden,
which by definition is
too heavy to carry
on your own.
—Unknown

I have a great friend. One that I absolutely adore. She is constantly tired and half the time sick. She wakes up at the crack of dawn only to retire almost 20 hours later. To say rest is limited is an understatement. She is a hard worker, and I'll never knock her for that. But a smart worker, maybe not so much. I have often offered to help with her overwhelming schedule at least a hundred times. Her response is always the same, "no thank you, I'm okay." It didn't take long for me to realize her fear of being a burden on others. The fear of the perception that she is incapable of managing her affairs and must now be rescued for the benefit of self. She needs an out for what she got in, and it will require means beyond her own and that's a hard pill to swallow. This friend of mine is no other than *Jacksina of All Trades Master of Nothing Betty* and she resides in most people I know and once took residence in my own soul.

L'EGGO OF MY EGO

Pride and ego are the ultimate stunters of growth. They cause us to think too much with too little. They are also what naturally stops us from asking for and receiving help. See we all have pride and ego, just in varying doses. Pride and ego are not bad attributes in moderation. You can take pride in your accomplishments knowing the hard work that it took to reach that plateau, however you cannot use that pride as a tool of insult for others who have not yet made such gains. You may have ego packaged in the form of confidence that allows you to develop into a leader, but you may not have so much that it interferes with your sincerity and doesn't attract followers. You may have pride enough where it forces you to find creative measures to surge past a struggle, but not so much that it clouds your judgement and limits the ability to accept needed support.

In our fictional scenario above, *Jacksina of All Trades Master of Nothing Betty* was ego driven and prideful. She was more interested in her successes being authored by self than being authored at all. Even though drowning in desire and over-whelmed by life, she could not pass by pride to accept genuine help from others. Help she so desperately needed. Pause Here. Is this you? Are you that single parent that turns down help so later you can gloat when telling your "I did this all by myself" stories? Even though you know people offered to help, and you didn't have to do it all by yourself. That was your choice. Is this you? If so, stop it! That is not attractive. We must always remember every great teacher was first a good student.

To grow into our desired selves, we must be humbled enough to know there's still much to learn. You never know what you don't know; so, being a student is a natural and constant progression of life. When we learn from others we allow them to dare I say it, help us. We allow them to broaden our horizons by increasing our knowledge which in turns opens our world to possibilities.

Accepting Help is NOT a Sign of Weakness

When I was little my parents introduced me to motivational speakers through tapes, videos, magazines, and television shows. Les Brown, Dexter Yager, and George and Ruth Housey were staples in our household. My parents were network marketers, and I'm an Amway brat. If anyone asked my siblings and I how we were, our immediate response *had to be* "we're GREAT!" True story. We could never say fine, or good. Always GREAT! Most of our family found that hilarious, but I think they get it now. Because my mother believed firmly that as long as you have breath, there's always the possibility of a great life. She would pack us up in the car and have my father whirl us around to different car dealerships and neighborhoods to dream. Long before I knew what a vision board was we had cutouts of Cadillac Sevilles and open house pics on the refrigerator. The Cadillac was for my dad and the house for my mother. I still have visions of the beige and white two story home in Parker Woods. That was her favorite.

They would then sit us down and talk about the family vision. What lied ahead for us? They would introduce us to six and seven figure success stories to remind my siblings and me just how close success was. Now while my parents never really hit any major levels in network marketing, they never honestly made what most would consider any real money; that exposure was powerful! Network marketing requires that you work with a team. Your success derives from your support system. Network marketing is rooted in the concept that it is a lot easier (and smarter) for one million people to do one thing each, than one person do a million things alone. Now, I'll tell you that as an adult I have tried my hand in the industry and never was able to gain traction. But the business and personal growth teachings offered in those circles was invaluable. Trying those business ventures out for myself reminded me of this simple truth—no one becomes successful alone. At some point, everyone needs help and accepting help is not a sign of weakness.

Self-Made Poverty Mentality

I cringe when I hear people speak about being "self-made" success stories. Oh, you may be a self-made *twentynaire*, or a self-made *hundred here and there*, but you will never be a self-made *million or billionaire*—IMPOSSIBLE!. It's like a unicorn, they don't exist. There's a huge difference between having your own and doing it on your own. Making it on your own is a poverty mentality, and those aiming for success surround themselves with mentors for this very reason. Listen to the stories of Oprah, Ariana Huffington, Steve Jobs, Walt Disney, Steve Harvey, or the person of your choosing that has reached a level of achievement undeniably deemed by most a success and hear what they have in common. NONE of them admit to doing it alone. They actually taunt the exact opposite.

HELP is not a dirty four letter word, so get you some.

"THANK YOU" IS ENOUGH

Confession, I have a bad habit. Actually I have a few bad habits, but don't judge me. I'm a work in progress. One bad habit I've had for years is the tendency of countering compliments with negatives. For example, let's say a friend says, "Oh I love your hair." I would respond with, "Girl you should of seen it yesterday, it was a hot mess." Or a business partner might comment, "Your presentation skills are awesome and polished." I would reply with, "A few years ago they were not, and I've had to really work on mastering the craft." Finally, I had a co-worker give me this wonderful advice. Just say *Thank*

You and hush up. Because we are close, I will tell you that I am MUCH better than I use to be, but I fall short now and then. I am learning to be a gracious receiver of all things, and you must learn this too. Whether it's a compliment or support we have to learn to say thank you, then, hush up.

In chapter 6 Wanted: Tribe Members, step 6:RECRUIT, I challenged you to build your tribe with key members to aid you in the journey to your best self, best family, best career, and best life. We had to think through who we knew and who we needed to meet in order to staff our tribe. Well, once our tribe is staffed, we have to allow them to fulfill the role for which they were selected. We have to be open to their ideas, suggestions, and efforts to enrich our lives. What's the purpose of recruiting people you don't plan to use? We have to be gracious receivers of their time and talents knowing that it is because of their efforts our lives are enhanced. We have to be ready at any moment to say "Thank You," then hush up. When you are a person with good intentions, favor is brought over you. Good people will be sent to you for the purpose of building your worth, building your family, building your career, and building your legacy. If we keep turning these people away, they are unable to fulfill their divine assignment and assist us with fulfilling ours. It's a lost-lost instead of a win-win.

Gracious Receiver

I worked in the public school system for 13 years with 11 of them being in the classroom. There was never a dull moment let me tell you! Kids are full of energy, humor, mischief, curiosity, and kindness. Contrary to what we may see in the media or hear in the neighborhood, our children are not a lost cause. But we better act now because it's getting harder and harder to rear them. I remember an 8th grade Georgia Studies Social Studies class that I taught at a Metro-Atlanta based middle school. That particular quarter most of my babies (I always refer to students as my babies) were struggling. They were just disconnected. I believe it may have been right before Spring Break, and the struggle was real. I offered to stay after school to do an extra study session with anyone interested to help prepare for the upcoming chapter test. Out of a class of 30, I had only three to take me up on the offer. They were three unlikely friends similar to the cast of the Breakfast Club, and they kept me going.

I must tell you that the first 30 minutes of our hour-long session had absolutely nothing to do with Georgia Studies. They wanted to talk and talk they did. I heard stories about marijuana high daddies, incarcerated mamas, current probation officer issues, home invasions gone wrong, who might be moving and changing schools (though they didn't want to go) soon. You name it, and they said it. I tell parents all the time to please know your kids are reporting ALL your business. Kids don't have filters. If you appear to have a listening ear, they will talk until advised not to do so. I knew this, but I also knew that kids don't care how much you know until they know how much you care. We can really take the "kids" away and simply say "people" don't care how much you know until they know how much you care. I knew that they had to get that conversation out of their system before I could teach them anything. It was way too many emotions built up that would interfere with the learning. That day became one of the very reasons I knew I had to leave the classroom and reach back to grab our parents. The behavior, character, or lack thereof that we see in class are a direct reflection of what happens in the home. I mean come on. Who can truly focus on Oglethorpe being the founder of Georgia when your mom is in jail? Now you and your siblings are thrown into the care of relatives you are not so fond of but told to proceed with life as normal. What?

So after our casual talk show style discussion, the real reason why I thought they stayed began. We reviewed and I broke down concepts to their bare bones. My babies' eyes opened, and they were hooked. Then I topped it off by giving them a cheat sheet that had all the answers to the upcoming test (not the actual test, but all the information). They were soooo excited. They were so grateful and gracious. I hooked them up! They never asked for my help, but when I offered it they accepted it. It was because of their acceptance of my help that they were able to release themselves of emotional burdens, and receive academic support. Without a doubt they had been enriched by the experience, and it all started with a willing spirit to accept an offer for support and not continue to struggle alone. How many of us have possibly missed out on a life enlightening and enriching opportunity because we couldn't get past our pride and ego enough to receive help? How many of us could really use unmeasurable favor being poured into our lives just for having a receiving spirit? How many? Because help is all around, we just have to be willing to accept it when it's offered.

BLESSINGS COMETH

Receive, Receive, Receive! Say it with me:

- I will be a gracious receiver of help.
- I will say "Thank You," then hush up
- I will not look at myself as lesser than for allowing others to be supportive of my mission or for accepting their talents to further my goals.
- I am not a burden, but I am an asset
- I will look for opportunities within the moment and seize them at every chance.
- HELP is not a dirty four-letter word, and I will seek it
- I am strong, I am capable, I am worthy of a victory, and I will not go it alone.

RECEIVE:

As parents, we are so accustomed to giving, giving, giving that it is sometimes uncomfortable to be on the receiving end. There's a balance that we must find and there is good on both sides.

Time to work:

1. Are there people in your life that have attempted to help you further life's goals and aspirations? Who?

2. What can these people help you accomplish?

3. When will you ask for their support (now that you are ready to receive it)?

4. Who else can you ask for help and how can they help you (maybe Tribe Members)?

One of the hardest parts about receiving help is relinquishing control enough to allow the giver to do their job. Make an effort to be a student and learn as much from the aider as possible. This attitude will take you far and advance you quicker.

We Will Beat and Redefine By...

RECEIVING

We will put ego and pride aside long enough to accept help. We will allow the people that we recruited as our support system to fulfill their role and do their job without interference. We will be open to new ways of thinking and problem solving. We will embrace that while *we can do all things*; we shouldn't, and will ask for wisdom to discern between the two. As GREAT parents we will teach our children that receiving help is not a sign of weakness, as long as the help is used for growth.

PART IV

ABOUT SUCCESS

NOTHIN' WRONG WITH CELEBRATING

The Lord's Prayer

Our Father,
which art in heaven
hallowed be thy name.
Thy kingdom come
thy will be done
in earth as it is in Heaven...
—Matthew 6:9-13 (KJV)

"Basically, I have to die to experience true happiness," I thought shaking my head in disbelief. From wee young ages children of the Christian faith are taught the Lord's Prayer, and I was no different. I remember feeling a sense of accomplishment once I mastered it, but then that was shattered when I realized various versions existed. "I have to learn those too," I thought. Funny, funny, and I was quickly assured that the one I knew was enough. One particular portion of the prayer resonated with me more than anything else, "in earth as it is in heaven." Now depending on the version of the prayer you're most familiar with, it may be worded "on earth," but for the sake of my argument either is acceptable. I was drawn to the line "in earth as it is in heaven" because of my grandmother's teachings and our disagreements.

GRANDMA VS. ME

Ms. Margaret Jones was your believer's believer. She was your textbook bible toting granny that knew the word like nobody's business. If you spent the night on Saturday, you better have some church clothes because it was going down on Sunday. No excuses. My grandmother was awesome and had a kind heart. She also had a delayed gratification belief that I didn't quite accept. I frequently heard my grandmother speak of getting your treasures in heaven. Riches beyond your imagination were waiting for the righteous in heaven. So do right, and be righteous so you can have it all later. While silver and gold, and flowers, and no more sickness, and smiling faces all sounded wonderful, I couldn't get past that line in the Lord's Prayer. Did it not say in earth as it is in heaven? Does that not mean some of those same opportunities for the heaven bound exist right here on this very earth on which we live? I don't know about you, but at a young age I knew I wasn't in any shape, fashion, or form interested in waiting on dying to enjoy *living*. It's time to celebrate! It is time to enjoy some of the perks of our existence while we are here "in earth."

EXHALE

Deep breathe in. Now hold it. Hold it. Exhale...ahhh. There's just something about exhaling that calms you. That release of breathe that lightens you. Yes, I could go into the scientific explanation of the process, but I choose to stay in my lane. I taught Language Arts and Social Studies. Please hold off on the science and math questions. But it works, right? You instantly feel better after doing it. At this point in our nine step transformation we have:

- **reflected** on life's experiences and our road to single
- worked on **resolving** our primary conflicts with self and others
- **reclaimed** our rightful role as leaders in our household and the captain of our journey
- **related** the circumstances to our children and are providing continuous support
- **recharged** our batteries by creating a clear vision for self and family with defining roles
- **recruited** our tribe of movers and shakers, big hearts, and thinkers to serve as our support system and guides on this journey to excellence
- graciously **received** help from those willing to propel our mission forward

Do you see how much work we've committed to doing in such a little time? WE ROCK! We are eight steps down in this nine step transformation. I just want you to take a moment to revel in how far you've come, how far we've come. Please don't make me go all Disney musical on you with the "We're All in This Together!" But we are, and look at the work we can do when we pull forces. Now work is part of the program. There is NO, I repeat, NO progress without work. Yes, some of the chapter questions require more time and effort than others. But life is a direct reflection of our efforts. So, how's it looking? If you cut corners with one of the steps, go back and get it done. This nine step program is a recipe and must be followed in order for best results. C'mon now. Would you flour the pan after you bake the cake? No. We can't always have it our way.

We have to retrain ourselves and break the habit of convenience. Everything in life doesn't necessarily come with a chronological flexibility plan. Some things you have to do in order to reap the most rewards. Now that we've done our due diligence, let's rejoice! We've worked hard. Be proud of the progress for perfection is a figment of our imagination. Let us always work toward progress and not perfection. Striving for an unattainable goal is simply exhausting! Who wants to be exhausted? We just exhaled. We want to be refreshed, spirit filled, recharged and ready to go. So pat yourself on the back and become the captain of your own cheer squad.

Joy is a decision,
a really brave one,
about how you are going to respond
to life.

—Wes Stafford

REWARD YOURSELF

I was one of those mamas that would go shopping and come back with bags of clothes for the kids and nothing for myself. I would run back and forth to practices and meetings and cancel anything that may have been for me be it a hair or nail appointment, or lunch with the girls. On every list I was last. When a parent, this is easy to do. Anyone been there? I *was*, but I'm not anymore. I had to learn from a girlfriend the benefits of rewarding yourself. You are no good to others if you aren't good to yourself first.

What I need you to do now is to treat yourself to something nice. Something you've wanted for a long time, but that doesn't make you have to recalculate all of this month's expenses. I want you to experience a no-guilt purchase as a show of gratitude for yourself and your efforts. Then capture the moment with a picture. Let that picture be a reminder of the road traveled and the progress made. Let it also remind you of the work to be done and the rewards ahead. Savor the moment. We are more inclined to continue a mission that has spirit "refill" stations along the way. Rewards offer that motivation, and the type of reward is up to your discretion, but makes it worth it so you are encouraged to repeat the behavior that earned it. In other words, don't skimp out. Make your purchase one that makes you a little uncomfortable, but you can live with. One of those, "because I'm worth it" purchases. I know all rewards aren't materialistic or cost money, but I need this particular reward to be tangible.

Fruits of Labor

After you have rewarded yourself, and only after, I want you to reward your children. Teach your children that good leads to good. Life is a product of decisions and efforts. We need to make sure our children see the struggle and the celebration to paint a more realistic picture of what life offers. Too frequently we attempt to shield our children from the ugly realities of consequences of actions and then wonder why their sense of entitlement exists. Let the babies know that because you are able to afford them the opportunity of reward as a result of the fruits of your labor. You completed a task, met your goal, and are making tremendous progress toward living your best life. By sharing these experiences, we model for our children the "sow before you reap" theory. I would also suggest that you come up with reward options from which they may choose. This sends the message that when you do the work you are in control. If they want to select the reward, they can do that once they have done the work and met one of their own goals.

Rejoicing, celebrating, and rewarding yourself are not selfish behaviors but positive deposits into the spirit. While there are still many miles to travel to complete transformation, just know that we are headed in the right direction. At times you may become uncomfortable, but growth comes from discomfort. So suck it up soldier and keep pressing. But in the meantime, keep celebrating your decision to take action and keep going!

STEP 8: REJOICE

The more you praise and celebrate your life,
the more there is in life to celebrate.
—unknown

Time to work:

1. Which step of the seven in this nine step transformational journey are you most proud of completing?

2. How do you plan to celebrate your accomplishment of completing seven of the nine steps outlined?

3. What three ways can you reward your child (ren) as recipients of the fruits of your labor?

4. Did you skip the "Time to work" portion of any of the steps introduced? If yes, go back and complete them before moving on to step nine, the final step. Always remember, there are no shortcuts to excellence. There may be multiple routes, but no *shortcuts*. The work must be done. Who loves ya? I DO!

We Will Beat and Redefine By...

REJOICING

We will take every step as a sign of progress and celebrate the effort. We will treat ourselves as royalty and not second-class citizens. We will not compete with the Joneses or the Kardashians in an effort to appreciate our own story. We will know that perfect people and perfect parents don't exist, so being GREAT is indeed enough. As GREAT parents we will teach our children the benefits of working hard and the rewards of such and how to enjoy those moments.

WORKED SO NICE I DID IT TWICE

Watch your thoughts,
For they become words.
Watch your words,
For they become actions.
Watch your actions,
For they become habits.
Watch your habits,
For they become character.
Watch your character,
For it becomes your destiny.

—Lao Tzu

E very morning for two school years I would hear the poem above recited over the intercom during morning announcements. It was the assistant principal's favorite poem that later became our school's mantra. She would often get on the intercom full of excitement and energy reminding the students' of the truth in the words. For two years, I would hear it, but wasn't listening to it. The essence of the poem was not understood until years later when I had an epiphany while reflecting on my life. I was at a place in life where I was, simply put, *tired*. I was tired of being on what I felt was a hamster wheel. I was moving, or existing and going nowhere at all. I had all these big dreams and had come to a point where I was making little to no progress on them.

FACEBOOK WAKEUP CALL

This was the same time I became social media curious. FaceBook was the thing so I began to spend countless hours stalking friends' profiles and becoming ever more envious of their "life." Now I know that everything people post online is not true, or at best a half-truth, but it got me thinking. Everyone is out here living it up and moving up, and I'm just here. Here, going through the days and appearing to be busy. But what am I really doing with my time? Better yet, what am I really doing with my talent? I was not one of those individuals that went through life trying to discover their talent. That I knew. I was given insight to my capabilities to communicate with the masses very early in life. The discovery of my purpose came a little later, but my talent I knew. While I was in the classroom teaching kids and broadening their horizons, I truly was not fully using my talent and it now made me sick to my stomach.

I wanted a lifestyle similar to my educated, careered friends online. They were happy, well-traveled, slim, polished, nice house, luxury cars, respected in their communities. Didn't I deserve that too? Then a flashback hit of a conversation I had with my mother about she and a longtime girlfriend that had started their adventures to adulthood at the same time. They both married (later divorced) and had kids, but one kept chasing her dream and the other didn't. As a result one became amongst the first black females to own a technology company and the other was my mother. While my mother was so proud of her friend, she couldn't help think how things could have been different if she would have kept pushing her purpose. I did NOT want my story to end like that. My mother has *many* accomplishments to be proud of, but she still often wonders about what could have been. I can't afford for that to be my story.

Consistently Inconsistent

Through reflection I was able to quickly identify the holes in my plan. I was inconsistent. I lacked discipline. How many of you have this problem? I had no problem getting started on a project; it was the continuation of it that destroyed my efforts. Let's face it. Most people fail because they are inconsistent. Successful people have a strong follow through game, and I was lacking there. Habits form character and character determines destiny. I finally got it. My inconsistency was a habit and one that had caused years of stunted growth. I then began to do what I advise everyone to do: study successful people. What do they do that others don't that allows them to continue to reach various plateaus?

HABITS WORTH FORMING

Here are my top 10 discoveries:

- They rise early: The early bird gets the job done.

- They plan out their day: Done the night before or first thing in the morning to stay focused

- They exercise: Not just for vanity, but for health reasons. It is hard to run an empire from a hospital bed.

- They pick an area to master: Doing everything is over-rated. They pick an industry in which to become an expert.

- They respect work life balance: They understand your career is what you do, not who you are. Have hobbies and multiple outlets.

- They constantly read: You can never know enough and change is inevitable. New strategies and techniques are always being developed that can help you with your craft.

- They surround themselves with success minded people: Lions travel with other lions.

- They are problem solvers: Everyone has a deficit so focus on your assets to solve the problem.

- They are optimist: Glass half full or running over
- They have a servant's spirit. "How can I help others? How can I improve someone's life?" They are philanthropic and volunteer time and money to charitable causes.

There are literally hundreds of articles and books about the habits of highly successful people, and I have easily read over fifty to date. The attributes mentioned are what I found to be the most common. My research allowed me to see that I was not making much progress in my life because I had too many focuses and that made it hard to consistently follow through with any of them. More and more studies are showing that multi-tasking is not only overrated, but destructive to our mental development and ability to concentrate. So the quality over quantity movement is back and we should get excited!

Successful people are intentional. It is through the repetition of proven behaviors (like the habits mentioned above) that they become and maintain a success.

THE NEW US

We, my friend, have made it to step nine of nine: Repeat. I am so proud of you for vesting an interest in strengthening your family by starting with self, that I can shout it from the rooftops! The road that led us here involved honest talk, evaluations, and plenty of action. This is just the beginning of our new forever and our new US. From this point on, it is unacceptable to retreat back to old ways of thinking. It is unacceptable to carry the load on our own. It is unacceptable to say and not do, to tell and not show. It is unacceptable to not forgive and move on. It is unacceptable to allow our circumstance to become our excuse. It is unacceptable not to dream, want more, and work for it. From now on, we are new and improved. We are the 2.0 version of self with a 3.0 debuting in the near future. We are taking the Apple approach to life with new upgraded models constantly being released as we continue to develop, to grow.

And Again

Like with any new product, there will be kinks. Doubt, fear, laziness, bad habits, the desire to be comfortable, expecting immediate results, prioritization issues, the lies about lack of time that we sell ourselves, the tired single parent cry of being a lone ranger, will all creep in at some point. That's to be expected. But what is also to be expected is your new reaction to such. How does the saying go? Life is 5% of what happens and 95% of how we react to it. We have a vision board, a mission statement, a plan of action, and a tribe to reference now to help us react appropriately and quickly. You will fall down. Heck, WE will fall down. We all do on this journey. It is the expectation. Without failure there is no success. Gather your tribe and put them on standby. As we journey to our best self, a strong support system is not only necessary, but a non-negotiable.

Most great people have attained
Their greatest success
Just one step beyond
Their greatest failure
—Napolean Hill

What separates losers from winners is how they react to failure. Does failure present a lesson from which to learn or a fatal end? Commit to getting back up as many times as it takes and keep working. If you find yourself stuck on a problem, I want you to go back through the nine steps:

- Reflect, how you got to the current state
- Resolve any personal or emotional ties to the problem
- Reclaim your composer and refocus to appropriately evaluate the problem
- Relate and reimagine equals working through the problem
- Recruit help if the problem is more than you can handle on your own due to limited ability, knowledge, and etcetera
- Receive help to fix the problem
- Rejoice to celebrate your accomplishment and repeat as many times as needed

The nine step process is not limited to single parent life evaluations. The formula works quite nicely for most problematic situations. So, when you find yourself stuck in any situation, go through the steps and work your way through it. I'm so excited and can't wait to meet you in your most authentic version of success. I'm so excited and can't wait to meet you (and your little people) in your most authentic version of success. You, my dear, ROCK and I thought that you should know

STEP 9: REPEAT

We are what we repeatedly do.

Time to work:

1. Have you ever experienced a wakeup call that prompted you to do more in life? If yes, what was it?

2. What three habits of highly successful people will you plan to adopt in the near future? Which one is the main priority?

3. What will be the first thing you do if things don't go as planned (remember that failure is never final)?

We Will Beat and Redefine By...

REPEATING

We will learn from the past, live in the present, and prepare for the future. We will look for patterns in our lives good and bad and make corrections as needed. We will apply the 9 steps as problems arise in a tailored form. We know that success comes from positive habits and habits are formed from constant practice= repeat, repeat, and repeat. No matter what, we will KEEP MOVING! As GREAT parents we will teach our children consistency and patience. Rome wasn't built in a day, and neither will our story, or our best life ever!

NEXT STEPS...

G-R-A, I want you to remember this. GRA= **G**et it, **R**ead it, **A**pply it. That's what this book is all about: getting it, reading it, and applying the information, discoveries, and action plans for your life. I don't want you to close it saying, "Now that was good reading! That Bishonna is a mess!" I want you to close this book with your next steps in mind. I don't want the pages of it to be pressed and polished, but folded, highlighted, and marked through. This is your Workbook and work is done in and outside of it. I also want this to become your GROWbook, and for you to experience massive growth because of it. When I visualized this product for us, I knew it couldn't go ultra-deep in any topic area. I wanted just enough to get our minds going and our bodies moving. It needed to be enough to prompt a move in a forward direction.

What I want for you is what you dream for your child, but once were afraid to chase for yourself. That form of excellence!

125

I want that for you. If I can help parents create a life for themselves that turns into a legacy for their children, I have fulfilled my purpose of saving families. Saving families doesn't equal me rescuing you from fires or bailing you out a financial hardship. No. Saving families for me is extensive but includes equipping you with the 9 step plan necessary to explore life's many opportunities. This enables you to make the best choices to create your most desired life. Our desires are limited by our exposures. The more we are exposed to, the ever more varied the possibilities.

Hopefully, my testimony has changed how you view "single parenting" and why we need to run from it. This job was not made for one. Help is needed and available if you *want it* and are willing to *seek it*. Help does not equal just a *spouse* people!

There is nothing wrong with being single, and there's nothing wrong with being a parent, but don't dare get caught up in the trap of using them together to encourage pity. We don't get to be the victim when our legacy is at stake. There's simply too much work to do to waste energy on that. To beat the odds and defy the stereotypes of single parenting, we have to redefine our destiny by not perpetuating the images associated with our presumed circumstances. When we change our reference and perception of self, we'll change the world's perception of us, and in turn of our offspring. Everyone has something that could be considered a deficit or a handicap that can hinder their ability to achieve, but it is only a deficit or a handicap if that is what YOU believe. Now continue this journey to excellence with the fervor and favor that only belongs to you, and I my dear, will see you at the next level soon!

ACKNOWLEDGMENTS

"Look, I did it!"

There are so many people to thank. Where do I start? My support system is phenomenal and the true definition of a blessing. My parents taught me to dream at a very young age and I never knew how powerful that was until I became an adult. I've always viewed the world as "I can have it" and the only thing that could ever stop me from getting it was me. Everyone wasn't taught that, yet this was my foundation. I thank you mom and dad for casting the net wide and allowing me to discover whatever I could imagine.

Mom, you were my first example of a single parent that did not use circumstance as a limitation. You kept going and made sure that every opportunity that was available to my peers was available to me. Even if that meant asking a *total stranger* to borrow their red corvette, because your baby needed a convertible for the homecoming parade. It didn't matter. No excuses. You did what you had to do to get the job done. I thank you for that and have embraced that attitude as part of my own parenting style.

Dad, I know exactly from where my love of writing stems and it's from you. The poetry that you exposed us to growing up was genius and I can't wait for the world to get a taste of it—officially. It's about time we introduce them to the father-daughter writing team.

To my brother and sisters-Mont, Nette, Carla, and Renae, thank you a million times over. Talk about pushing each other to reach for more. What a bond we share. All those times you got on my nerves and I wanted to be an only child, I take back. This milestone happened with your help and is just one chapter of the Jones Kids' Story. So proud of us and our families and what we've done over the years and what we have in the works.

The Colbert Family, we are living proof of the village theory. When I tell people how my in-laws (can't say ex-in laws because that just sounds weird) are my lifeline they are in disbelief! The type of relationship we have is one envied by most and described as a desirable at Sunday morning service. Jerry, we co-parent better now divorced than we ever did married! Funny how that works, but it does indeed work and quite well. Up top buddy!

The girlfriend crew from high school, to college, to work, I want to say "Yeah Chicas!" You guys rock and have always made me feel like I could be Oprah if so desired. Thank you over and over. It's great to have solid confidants in your corner and dancing on top of the table depending on the circumstances.

Shout out to my book squad! All the technical people that helped put this together. Thank you Genine Bonaby for editing, Kaneisha Harris, Renae Jones, and Ayanna Horton for proofing, Kevin Ogle for photography and cover design, Tony Gaskins for author coaching, and Ghislain Viau for formatting. For a freshman piece I think we did alright. Something to be proud of indeed.

Last but certainly not least, THANK YOU GOD! I will never be ashamed to tell people I am one of your children and that I will follow you anywhere. From these years on this earth I have discovered that you sure do have a sense of humor, but relentless patience as well. Thank you for choosing me to be the vessel for this message and many more. Should I tell them what we have cooking? Naw, let's make'em wait.

To everyone near and far who have supported me on this journey, a very sincere—THANK YOU!

Better Us=Better Them   Time to save families!

SugarFreely,

Bishonna

ABOUT THE AUTHOR

Bishonna Jones, *The School Messenger,* is a veteran educator, speaker, and founder of the SugarFree Parenting Movement. Jones has worked with thousands of families over the last decade on the topics of personal development, education, and community activism and resources. Recognized by the Georgia Department of Education and multiple institutions for contributions to advance family and community engagement, Jones continues to captivate audiences with her real, relevant, and results-oriented approach to thriving and parenting in the millennium. www.bishonnajones.com

57262845R00087

Made in the USA
Charleston, SC
11 June 2016